THE STATUE OF LIBERTY

A TRUE BOOK

by

Patricia Ryon Quiri

Children's Press®
A Division of Scholastic Inc.

New York Toronto London Auckland Sydney
Mexico City New Delhi Hong Kong
Danbury, Connecticut

Reading Consultant
Linda Cornwell
Learning Resource Consultant
Indiana Department
of Education

Author's Dedication:
For my dear friend and
colleague Jill Granstrom.
You are special, Willie.
Love, P.Q.

Library of Congress Cataloging-in-Publication Data

Quiri, Patricia Ryon.
    The Statue of Liberty / by Patricia Ryon Quiri.
        p.   cm. — (A true book)
    Includes bibliographical references and index.
    Summary: Recounts how the Statue of Liberty was planned, built, dedi-
cated, repaired over the years, and then restored in the 1980s.
    ISBN 0-516-20628-1 (lib. bdg.)   0-516-26385-4 (pbk.)
    1. Statue of Liberty (New York, N.Y.)—Juvenile literature. 2.
Bartholdi, Frédéric Auguste, 1834-1904—Juvenile literature. [1. Statue
of Liberty (New York, N.Y.) 2. National monuments. 3. Statue.]   I.
Title. II. Series
F128.64.L6Q57   1998
974.7'1—dc21   97-12216
                                                                      CIP
                                                                       AC

CHILDREN'S PRESS, and A TRUE BOOK®, and associated logos are
trademarks and or registered trademarks of Scholastic Library Publishing.
SCHOLASTIC and associated logos are trademarks and or registered
trademarks of Scholastic Inc.

12 13 14 15 16 17 18 19 20 R 10 09 08 07

Contents

An Old Friendship

The United States of America became a free and independent country in 1783. This had not come easily for the people of the United States. They had to fight a war against Great Britain called the Revolutionary War. They fought this war with the help of many people from France.

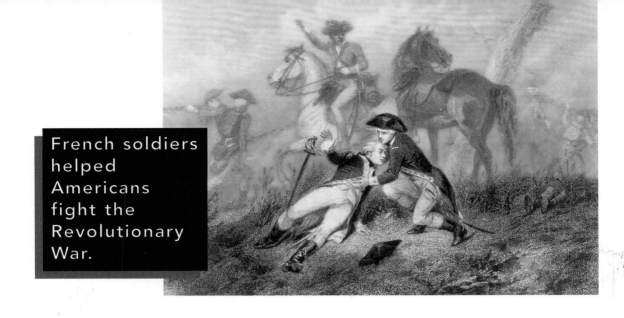

French soldiers helped Americans fight the Revolutionary War.

A strong friendship grew between the United States and France. Many people from France liked the way the American government was run. They hoped that France could have a similar government someday. Like Americans, the French felt that freedom was very important.

A Colossal Plan

In 1865, nearly one hundred years after the United States won its independence, a group of Frenchmen were having dinner at the home of Edouard de Laboulaye. He lived near Versailles, France. He knew a lot about the United States. He admired the young country and what it stood for—liberty and freedom. He wanted

France to have the same sort of government.

Because many people of France shared the same ideas as Americans, the men at Laboulaye's house felt that there was a special feeling, or bond, between the two countries. Laboulaye thought France should give a gift to the United States. He thought a huge statue symbolizing American independence would be a wonderful gift.

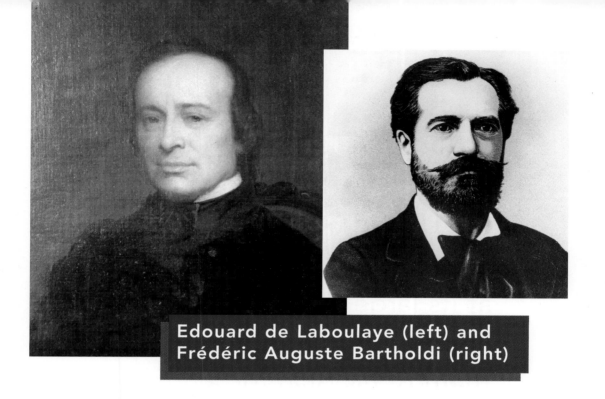

Edouard de Laboulaye (left) and
Frédéric Auguste Bartholdi (right)

Frédéric Auguste Bartholdi
was a young sculptor who was
at the dinner party. He had
been making statues for many
years. He loved the idea of
making a giant-sized statue
for the United States.

Six years later, Frédéric Auguste Bartholdi traveled to the United States. He traveled all over the country, amazed at its large size. He met many important people and told them of his plan for a huge statue. Many people were interested in the plan.

Bartholdi made many friends in the United States, including a Frenchwoman named Jeanne-Emilie Baheux de Puysieux. They became

Jeanne-Emilie
Baheux de Puysieux

good friends and eventually,
they married.

While in America, Bartholdi
discovered the perfect spot
for his statue. There was a little
island right at the front of New
York Harbor. It was called
Bedloe's Island. During the War

of 1812, Fort Wood had been built on the island. The fort had been built in the shape of a star, and it was still there. The statue could be placed within the star-shaped walls.

The statue would be of a woman holding a torch high in the air. Bartholdi would call her "Liberty Enlightening the World." She would represent Libertas, Ancient Rome's goddess of free-dom. People arriving in New York Harbor by ship would be

Bartholdi thought his statue could be built inside the walls of the old fort on Bedloe's Island.

THE GREAT BARTHOLDI STATUE,
LIBERTY ENLIGHTENING THE WORLD.
THE GIFT OF FRANCE TO THE AMERICAN PEOPLE.
TO BE
ERECTED ON BEDLOE'S ISLAND, NEW YORK HARBOR.

The statue of bronze, 148 ft in height, is to be mounted on a stone pedestal 150 ft high, making the extreme height 298 ft. The torch will display a powerful electric light, and the statue thus present by night as by day, an exceedingly grand and imposing appearance.

welcomed by this "Statue of Liberty."

Bartholdi did not start working on his statue until

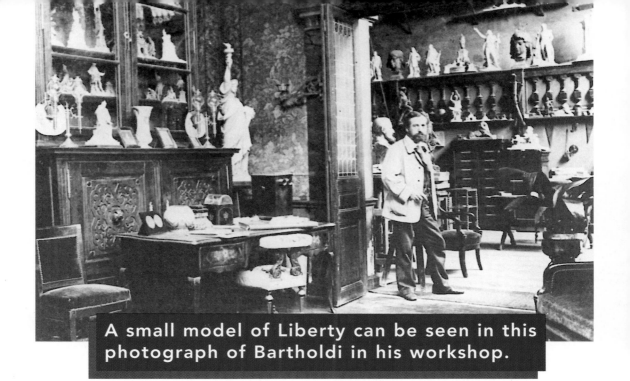

A small model of Liberty can be seen in this photograph of Bartholdi in his workshop.

1876. He rented a large workshop and began his project. He first made a 4-foot (1.2-meter) clay model of a woman in a long Roman gown. Her right hand held a torch high in the air. The torch meant that she

14

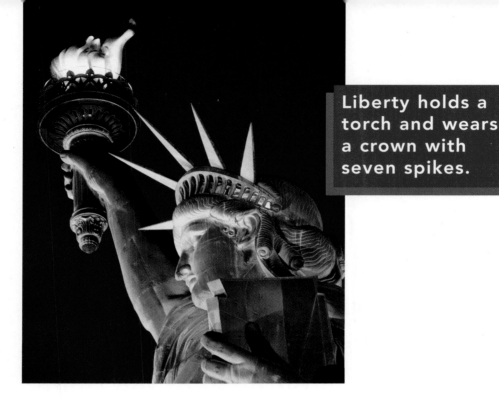

Liberty holds a torch and wears a crown with seven spikes.

was "enlightening the world." Around her head was a crown with seven spikes. This crown symbolized her divine nature. Some say the seven spikes stood for the seven continents and seven seas of the world.

Bartholdi put a broken chain at her feet. The broken chain symbolized America's newly won freedom from Great Britain. The statue's face was serious. In her left hand she held a tablet. On the tablet was the birthday of the United States: July 4, 1776. This was written in Roman numerals.

Bartholdi then made a 9-ft. (2.7-m) model and a 36-ft. (11-m) model. Bartholdi's mother posed for her son. He used her as a model for Liberty's face.

"July 4, 1776" is written in Roman numerals on a tablet in Liberty's left arm (left). Bartholdi's mother (top right) was the model for Liberty's face (bottom right).

He used his friend Jeanne-Emilie as a model for Liberty's body. Soon, work began on the full-sized statue.

Who Will Pay for Such a Statue?

The French people raised money to pay for the statue. In the United States, people raised money to pay for the pedestal, or base, of the statue. Some people in the United States thought that France should pay for the whole thing.

A poster for an event to raise money for the statue's pedestal

Others thought that the statue and pedestal were really just for New York, and that New Yorkers should have to pay for them. But soon people became convinced that this was a statue for the whole country, not just the people of New York. It was a statue that represented freedom for everyone. As it turned out, many people throughout the country, including schoolchildren, sent in money to help pay for the project.

Building Lady Liberty

Building such a huge statue was done slowly. Hundreds of people worked on the project. They listened to Bartholdi as he explained how he wanted it done. The statue was going to be so big that it would never fit in the workshop. For example, the length of her arm

would be 42 ft. (13 m). The index finger alone was going to be 8 ft. (2.4 m) long. The mouth was going to be 3 ft. (0.9 m) wide.

Because the statue would be so colossal, it had to be built in sections. First the workers made full-sized models of pieces of the statue by covering huge wooden frames with plaster. Then they built wooden molds that followed the outside shape of the plaster models. Thin copper sheets were hammered into each mold. Eventually, the copper sheets would be placed on a steel framework, or "skeleton," and attached to one another to form an entire statue.

Workers hammering copper sheets into wooden molds to create sections of Liberty's "skin"

Bartholdi used copper because it was light and strong. He thought copper would last well in the salty air of the New York harbor. It was also less expensive than other metals.

The statue would be made up of three hundred sections.

The first part to be built was the right arm and torch. Bartholdi's workers started on this part because it was going on display in Philadelphia at the big Centennial exposition. When it was finished in May 1876, it was put in twenty-one crates and shipped by boat to the United States.

Liberty's head was completed in 1878. It, too, went on display, in Paris, France. Both Liberty's head and torch raised money to help pay for the

The right arm on display in Philadelphia in 1876 (left) and Liberty's head on display in Paris in 1878 (right)

statue. People could pay money to climb into each part of the statue.

Bartholdi Gets Help

Bartholdi got the help of a famous bridge builder, a Frenchman named Gustave Eiffel. Eiffel designed the inner support—a "skeleton" framework—for the Statue of Liberty. He later designed the Eiffel Tower in Paris, France.

Gustave Eiffel designed Liberty's iron-and-steel framework.

By 1884, the Statue of Liberty was finished. It stayed in Paris until the next year. Then Bartholdi and his workers took it apart piece by piece and shipped it to the United States.

A photo (left) of the statue being built in Paris and construction of the statue's pedestal (above)

Another man who helped with the project was an American named Richard Morris Hunt. He designed the pedestal—the base on which Liberty would stand.

Through his newspaper, Joseph Pulitzer helped raise money for the statue's pedestal.

Joseph Pulitzer, publisher of a New York newspaper, was very helpful in raising money for the pedestal. His paper printed the names of all the people who gave money to the Statue of Liberty fund.

Liberty Sets Sail

On May 21, 1885, the Statue of Liberty was ready to sail to her new home on Bedloe's Island. It took four months to pack the statue into 214 crates! A French naval ship called the *Isère* carried the crates containing the statue across the Atlantic Ocean. It took about

The *Isère*, carrying all the pieces of the statue, arrives in New York Harbor (left). Workers constructed the statue's head last (right).

four weeks. The statue was to be put together again in her new home on Bedloe's Island in New York Harbor. The Statue of Liberty would face the ocean, welcoming people as they came by ship.

October 28, 1886, finally arrived! This was the day the Statue of Liberty would be dedicated to the people of the United States. A big ceremony was planned. It was a cold and rainy morning, and a little foggy, but the weather didn't stop the crowds from watch-ing. People lined the streets of New York City for the biggest

On October 28, 1886, the Statue of Liberty was unveiled.

parade ever. Others watched Bedloe's Island from their boats. Bartholdi was all the way up in the statue's crown. He was waiting for a signal to let down the French flag that covered Liberty's face. Thinking that a speech by Senator William Evarts was finished, he let down the flag. The speech really wasn't over, but it was too noisy for the senator to continue.

President Grover Cleveland was also at the dedication and gave a speech as well. This was a proud day for all American and French people. But it was an especially proud day for Frédéric Auguste Bartholdi!

Repairs for Lady Liberty

Over the years, the Statue of Liberty has needed repairs. In 1933, President Franklin Roosevelt gave the care of the Statue to the Office of National Parks, Buildings, and Reservations. The name of this agency was changed to the National Park Service the next

Problems like rust (right) meant that Liberty needed a major repair job by the 1980s (left).

year. This agency spent money on needed repairs to Liberty.

Major fundraising began in 1984 for repairs to Liberty for her one-hundredth birthday. Big businesses, individuals, and once again, schoolchildren, raised money. Scaffolding completely surrounded Liberty so

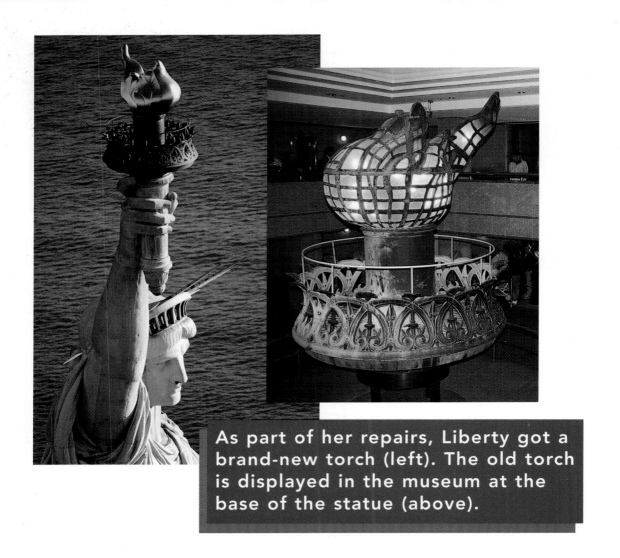

As part of her repairs, Liberty got a brand-new torch (left). The old torch is displayed in the museum at the base of the statue (above).

workers could make repairs. Included in the repairs was a new torch for Liberty.

Liberty's one-hundredth-birthday celebration in 1986

Visiting the Statue of Liberty

Because it is on an island, visitors to the statue arrive by ferryboat. The statue is about 305 ft (about 93 m) high from base to torch. Visitors can also visit the Liberty Museum exhibit, located under the statue's pedestal.

**Visitors travel to the Statue
of Liberty by ferry.**

Another place to visit on
the island is a sculpture gar-
den. Statues of the people
who were important in the

Statue of Liberty's history—
Bartholdi, Laboulaye, Eiffel,
Lazarus, and Pulitzer—are in
this area.

Emma Lazarus

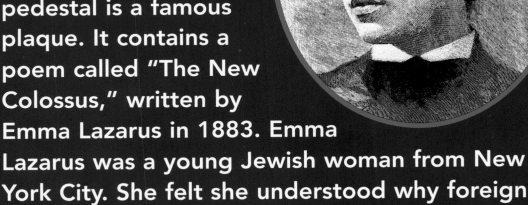

Inside Liberty's pedestal is a famous plaque. It contains a poem called "The New Colossus," written by Emma Lazarus in 1883. Emma Lazarus was a young Jewish woman from New York City. She felt she understood why foreign people move to the United States. She believed they moved in search of liberty and freedom. Her poem is written as if Liberty herself is speaking. Here are the poem's best-known words:

> Give me your tired, your poor,
> Your huddled masses yearning to breathe free,
> The wretched refuse of your teeming shore;
> Send these, the homeless, tempest-tost to me,
> I lift my lamp beside the golden door!"

To Find Out More

Here are some additional resources to help you learn more about the Statue of Liberty:

 **Books**

Coerr, Eleanor. **Lady with a Torch.** Harper & Row, 1986.

Haskins, Jim. **The Statue of Liberty: America's Proud Lady.** Lerner Publications, 1986.

Krensky, Stephen. **Maiden Voyage: The Story of the Statue of Liberty.** Atheneum, 1985.

Miller, Natalie. **The Statue of Liberty.** Children's Press, 1992.

Organizations and Online Sites

Great Outdoor Recreation Pages (GORP):
Statue of Liberty National Monument
http://www.gorp.com/gorp /resource/US_nm/ny_liber. htm

History of the Statue of Liberty, visitor information, and lots of links.

Hot Links
http://www.ellisisland.org/

Great links to Statue of Liberty- and Ellis Island-related sites.

Statue of Liberty and Ellis Island
http://fieldtrip.com/ny/236 37620.htm

History and information on the Statue of Liberty and Ellis Island.

Statue of Liberty National Monument and Ellis Island
Liberty Island
New York, NY 10004
http://www.nps.gov/stli

This organization runs two exciting places to visit: the Ellis Island Immigration Museum and the Statue of Liberty. Its website offers history, stories, statistics, and photos about Ellis Island and the Statue of Liberty.

Important Words

colossal huge

divine having to to with God or a god

enlighten to inform

exposition large public display of art or industry

immigrant person who leaves one country to settle in another

independent self-governing; free

refuse worthless things

scaffold temporary structure put up to support workers while they repair a sculpture or building

tablet sheet of metal, wood, or stone with words or designs written on it

tempest violent storm

Index

Meet the Author

Patricia Ryon Quiri lives in Palm Harbor, Florida, with her husband Bob and their three sons. Ms. Quiri graduated from Alfred University in upstate New York and has a B.A. in elementary education. She currently teaches second grade in the Pinellas County School system. Other True Books by Ms. Quiri include *Ellis Island*, *The American Flag*, *The National Anthem*, and *The Bald Eagle*.